Sandra Haydee Giroux

Always, Forever Friends

A Journey of Unbreakable Love

By Sandra Haydee Giroux

Cover image: Rusty (Left) kissing Heidi

Sandra Haydee Giroux

Paperback ISBN: 979-8-9930101-2-0

Dedication:

To Rusty and Heidi, who taught me that love doesn't sit still, it leaps, barks, and stays close.
To every soul who loves a dog, and to the One who whispered this story into being—this is for you.

Sandra Haydee Giroux

Introduction

This story is real—well, about 98% real. The names, the places, the muddy paws, and midnight cuddles all come from life with Rusty Papito, a dog whose heart is as big as his bark is small. What began as a few stories shared with friends became a trail of memories, each one a reminder of how deeply animals shape our lives.

Rusty is more than a companion. He is a teacher, a protector, and a friend whose loyalty never wavers. And he isn't alone. Heidi, his spirited sister and partner in mischief, shaped his life and ours in ways we're still discovering. Together, they continue to teach us about joy, resilience, and the quiet magic of being truly seen.

These tales are not just about them—they're about the comfort of shared silence, the laughter in everyday moments, and the kind of friendship that stays with you, always.

I hope these pages bring you smiles, maybe a few tears, and the feeling that you've met someone truly special.

AI generates some of the pictures, while others are real.

Chapter One

The Deal

The morning was cold in Maniba, a quiet country town in Pennsylvania. A little puppy slept peacefully, nestled against his mother's warm abdomen, unaware that today would mark the beginning of a new chapter.

Inside the house, a couple—husband and wife—were preparing to send off the last puppy of the litter to his new owner in Florida.

At 5:15 a.m., a knock at the door stirred the household. The man of the house greeted the stranger who had come to take Toby away from his biological and human family. It was too early for the little one to be awake, and as unfamiliar arms lifted him, adrenaline surged through his tiny body.

Toby squirmed, trying to escape the stranger's grasp, but his efforts were gentle and futile. In a hurry, he was placed into a crate waiting in the van, alongside other dogs already tucked inside their own compartments.

Documents and payment were exchanged between the visitor and the couple, and then the van pulled away. Each time it stopped to pick up another dog, a chorus of barks erupted, making Toby even more nervous. The world outside was changing fast—and he didn't yet know what it all meant.

Where Are We Going?

Where are they taking me?
Mom? Dad? Please help me!

But no one came to his rescue. Invisible tears rolled down his furry cheeks. He had never worn a collar, felt the tug of a leash, or seen the inside of a crate. Vehicles were foreign to him—though he had heard their engines rumble in the distance, always followed by the mysterious disappearance of one of his siblings.

Toby was an innocent puppy, raised in the quiet countryside. All he had known was the lush greenery around him and the love of a family who lived a simple life in a remote town, surrounded by nature.

His siblings were gone, one by one, and he never understood why. He had felt unique, even lucky, to remain with his parents. And he truly was.

The van arrived at its destination: the airport.

The Flight

Toby stirred and, noticing daylight outside, peeked through the slats of his kennel. He saw that all the dogs were being unloaded and taken into a large warehouse.

Where are they taking us? he wondered, his thoughts trembling with uncertainty.

The unexpected, heart-wrenching journey was beginning to weigh on him, and anxiety crept in like a shadow.

After some time, the dogs were moved again—this time to a large aircraft bound for a new place, one we would come to call home. The cargo hold was pressurized, and the soft, rumbling sound of the engines, coupled with the steep incline during take-off, gave all the dogs a rush of adrenaline. Most were young and experiencing this journey for the first time, their nerves heightened by the unfamiliar motion. Eventually, the steady ride and lack of stimulation lulled them into sleep.

Toby could only think of home—playing with his siblings, his mom and dad, the meals his owners lovingly prepared each day, and the peaceful, problem-free life he'd known in the countryside.

After a few hours, a subtle sense of descent stirred all the passengers. Nervousness settled in as they pondered their next steps. The plane had a scheduled two-hour layover in a city before continuing to its final destination.

The flight was mostly uneventful—until a brief bout of turbulence jolted everyone on board. Screams echoed from the cabin, though the dogs, unable to hear them, expressed their anxiety with barks that sounded like pleas for help. The sudden shaking heightened their unease.

When the crates rattled, Toby whimpered. A gentle paw touched his side.

"Don't worry, kid," said a voice. "We're all in this together."
Soon after, the plane touched down in Tampa, Florida.

Toby' Arrival in Tampa

It was 2:00 in the afternoon on December 30—wintertime across the country. The weather in Tampa was cool and breezy, far milder than the biting cold of the place Toby had left behind.

The dogs in their crates were the first to disembark, carried into a warehouse where their new owners would soon arrive. Most barked loudly, their voices echoing through the space, but Toby remained quiet—scared and confused.

Though food and water had been provided, he hadn't touched either. Even the training pad lining his kennel was dry. He had been holding it in for hours, instinctively resisting the unfamiliar. In his silent protest, he had imposed a fast on himself, leaving him slightly weakened.

Art, the puppy's new owner, anxiously scanned the rows of kennels—thirty in total—lined up in the receiving area like silent sentinels. His eyes darted from tag to tag, searching for the one with his name.

When he finally found it, his heart skipped. The crate appeared empty. He crouched down, concern tightening in his chest, and peered inside.

There, in the far corner, was a tiny figure—smaller than he had imagined—timidly pressed against the wall of the crate. The puppy's eyes met his for a fleeting moment before darting away. Relief washed over Art, mingled with a surge of protectiveness.

For a month, Art had been watching the puppy's listing online, drawn to his timid eyes and quiet demeanor. After weeks of deliberation, he finally made the decision: this was the one.

Now, with a grin stretching across his face, he wheeled the crate out of the warehouse and gently secured it in the back seat of his car. Toby remained curled in the corner, still too overwhelmed to move.

Before starting the engine, Art paused. The puppy might need to relieve himself after the long journey. He opened the crate and reached in slowly, speaking in a soft voice. Toby flinched at first, but allowed himself to be lifted.

Art cradled the tiny body in his arms and reached for the collar he'd brought—sized for a dog between fifteen and twenty pounds.

Toby, barely seven pounds and still trembling, stood uncertainly on the seat as Art fastened the oversized collar loosely around his neck, careful not to startle him.

The Escape

In the cargo area parking lot, Art gently placed Toby on the ground and led him toward a patch of grass for a short walk. The puppy sniffed the air, his body tense, eyes darting in every direction.

Surrounded by delivery trucks and trailers, the space felt loud and unfamiliar. Driven by survival instincts, Toby quickly surveyed the surroundings—then, in a flash, slipped free of the oversized collar and leash. Before Art could react, the tiny creature bolted, disappearing beneath a large truck parked nearby.

Heart pounding in panic, Art sprinted after him, scanning the shadows under each vehicle. He dropped to his knees, crawling and peering beneath bumpers and axles, calling softly.

Finally, under the wide frame of a pickup, he spotted Toby— curled beside a massive tire, trembling and breathless, his small chest rising and falling in rapid bursts.

Art circled around the truck and, stretching his arm beneath the chassis, carefully reached for the trembling puppy. His fingers closed gently around Toby's small body, securing him before he could make another dash.

He lifted him slowly and cradled him against his chest, the puppy's fragile frame pressed against his shoulder. With no choice but to accept his fate, Toby wrapped one leg around Art's neck while the other rested limply on his chest. His chin settled on Art's shoulder, and his eyes—heavy with sadness—gazed into the distance.

For the next two hours, Toby traveled in his crate, silent and still, as they made their way to Ocala, a city nestled between country farms and the hum of a growing business community. It was a place of quiet roads and open skies, where Art hoped healing might begin.

Sandy Meets Rusty

At home, Sandy—Art's wife—was eagerly awaiting the arrival of their new puppy. They had already chosen a name for him: Rusty.

Though she was still recovering from surgery a month earlier, Sandy felt strong enough to care for the little one. Her anticipation had grown with each passing hour.

When Art stepped through the kitchen door, Rusty nestled on his shoulder, Sandy's eyes lit up. Art turned slightly, revealing the puppy's face. When she first saw the puppy, something inside her shifted. She didn't just fall in love—she connected with him in a way that defied explanation. Rusty had etched himself into her soul. His eyes, wide and searching, held a quiet vulnerability that mirrored something in her own heart. As Art gently placed him in her lap, she felt a warmth bloom in her chest —a sense of recognition, as if they had always belonged to each other. Art smiled, sensing the silent exchange between them, and the room seemed to hush around that moment, as if time itself paused to witness the beginning of something sacred. It felt less like a beginning and more like a reunion. In that moment, she knew: this little creature wasn't just a pet—he was a companion, a witness, a piece of her story.

He was the most adorable little ball of brown fur she had ever seen. His almond-shaped eyes, a soft shade of light brown, held a transparent glow—beautiful and haunting, touched by sadness and fatigue.

His fur was about two inches long, silky and tousled. The hair on his forehead swept gently back, as if someone had been stroking it for comfort during a long, uncertain journey.

Emotional Moment

Art showed her how to cradle him like a baby, his tiny head resting on her shoulder, one little paw curled around her collarbone as if holding on for dear life. He was a mini Aussie Doodle—soft, delicate, and impossibly small. Now, at last, they had the dog they had long dreamed of.

At first, he refused food or water. He wanted nothing more than to sleep, nestled in his mommy's arms, wrapped in the safety of her heartbeat. She held him close, barely breathing, afraid to disturb the fragile peace he had found.

When he woke a couple of hours later, his eyes fluttered open with quiet trust. Art offered him a few drops of plain yogurt from the tip of his finger, and Rusty accepted them slowly, as if tasting the world for the first time.

For Sandy, that moment held more than tenderness, it awakened something long dormant. She hadn't had children of her own, but as she cradled Rusty, she felt the fullness of maternal love rise within her. This tiny creature, so vulnerable and pure, had unlocked a part of her heart she hadn't known was waiting. He wasn't just a puppy. He was her baby.

FIRST DAY
together

FIRST DAY
together

The beginning of a furry love story

Chapter Two

Rusty's First Trip to the Dog Park

Just a few hours after bringing Rusty home, Art—despite feeling tired—suggested they take him to the community dog park. He and Sandy loaded Rusty into their golf cart and drove through the quiet neighborhood, the evening air soft and welcoming.

When they arrived, the park was empty, its wide fenced space silent and still. They gently placed Rusty in the center of the enclosure. He sat up straight, ears perked, eyes darting from left to right and all around. His little body buzzed with excitement.

Yippee! Yay! I love this! he seemed to cheer in his mind, soaking in the open space and the promise of adventure.

Rusty Becomes the Park's Joyful Greeter

The next day at the park, Rusty began to notice the rhythm of things—people arriving with dogs on leashes, each pair connected by a quiet bond. Small dogs headed to the small park, big ones to the larger space. Rusty watched it all with wide-eyed wonder, studying the interactions between owners and pets, and among the dogs themselves. He loved them all.

Through the gaps in the chain-link fence, he would approach passing dogs, sticking out his tiny tongue in playful greeting—offering kisses to strangers with fearless affection. Even at a young age, Rusty became the park's unofficial greeter, winning hearts with his charm and gentle spirit.

It didn't take long before he began doing his zoomies—wild, joyful sprints around the park that left the other small dogs chasing after him in delight. He was the fastest, the happiest, and the spark that lit up the space. Soon, he had a circle of furry friends among the regulars, and the humans formed bonds of their own, united by laughter and shared stories.

His mom took him to the park three times a day, every day, during her leave from work. It became his joyful routine—a rhythm of play, friendship, and freedom that shaped his early days in Ocala.

Rusty and Sandy Bond Through Play

But at home, Rusty was timid and quiet by nature. During his first week at home, he often sat on a rug with his toys, content to observe his surroundings. Sandy would join him there, gently teasing him by waving her hand over his head, coaxing him to play. Rusty responded with delight, and from that moment on, they became inseparable playmates.

He developed a charming habit of nudging her leg—sometimes even wrapping his paws around it in a playful plea for more playtime. It was his quirky little signal, full of affection and excitement. Whenever Rusty got especially thrilled, he'd let out an adorable growl—a soft, rumbling sound that became his signature expression of joy during their games.

Through these moments, Rusty's bond with Sandy deepened. Play became their language, and joy their rhythm.

Rusty's First Night of Freedom

Little Rusty had slept in a crate in his new parents' bedroom for about a month, until he was fully house-trained. He was quiet through the night and had learned to hold it until morning. Each day, Art would gently carry him out on his shoulder to go to the bathroom— a tender routine that helped Rusty grow into a confident, independent little dog.

Eventually, Art knew it was time. Rusty had earned their trust.

One evening, the three of them were in the family room—Art and Sandy reading in their chairs, Rusty curled up in his bed in the corner. When it was time to retire for the night, Art made a quiet decision. He left Rusty sleeping peacefully in his bed and didn't bring him to the crate.

The next morning, Rusty woke up and blinked in astonishment. He was still in his bed—no crate, no confinement. He couldn't believe it. Quietly, he padded into the master bedroom and saw Mom and Dad still asleep, the crate sitting empty beside their bed.

Mom? Dad? Is this real? Will I not be sleeping in the crate anymore?

16

The well-behaved little dog had proven himself. From that day on, Rusty was free to roam the house—a trusted companion, no longer bound by barriers, but by love alone.

Eventually, Rusty was allowed to sleep with Mom and Dad. In Sandy's culture, dogs weren't typically permitted on the bed, so when Art placed Rusty there one afternoon—"just" to play with him on his chest—Sandy instinctively prepared to object. But something about the scene stopped her: the tenderness in Art's gesture, the way Rusty nestled into the moment as if he belonged. She said nothing. Instead, she welcomed the little creature onto the bed, recognizing the quiet shift in their shared life. And knowing Art's intentions, she allowed Rusty to sleep with them—not under the covers, but close enough to feel the warmth of belonging.

That night, as Rusty curled up at the foot of the bed, Sandy lay still, listening to his soft breaths. It was a small creature, barely the size of a small pillow, yet his presence filled the room with something unspoken. She thought about the rules she had grown up with, the invisible lines between humans and animals, and how love—unexpected and unassuming—had begun to blur them. Art hadn't asked for permission; he had simply followed his heart. And Sandy, moved by the purity of that gesture, let go of the old boundaries. Rusty wasn't just a dog anymore. He was family.

Rusty's Nose Knows & His Heart Follows

From an early age, Rusty had a remarkable gift: he could spot a female dog being walked on a leash from what felt like a mile away. His whole body would light up with excitement, and he'd pull with all his might to run toward her—his mission clear and heartfelt: deliver a kiss.

Under optimal conditions—clear skies, open paths, and no obstructions—dogs can detect scents from astonishing distances. Some studies suggest they can smell as far as 20 kilometers (12.4 miles), and when it comes to a female dog in heat, their olfactory powers are even more impressive—up to 3 miles away. Rusty's nose was no exception. His instincts were finely tuned, and his heart followed wherever his nose led.

When he wasn't at the dog park, his mom would take him for walks along the winding community pathways. But Rusty didn't walk—he flew.

Yay! I love chasing the wind, Mom! It's so much fun! Hurry up! he would exclaim with every tug of the leash.

"Slow down, Rusty! Please slow down!" his mom would plead, trying to keep pace. But Rusty didn't understand the concept of walking. He only knew the thrill of running freely in nature, the wind in his fur and the world unfolding before him.

He wore a collar and leash, but his mom worried. His joyful sprints often turned into powerful pulls, and she feared he might choke himself in his eagerness. The collar would tighten, and his exuberance would turn into strained gasps that made her wince. Eventually, they got him a harness—a simple adjustment that brought a wave of relief. No more choking, no more coughing fits— just Rusty, trotting proudly beside them, his joy undiminished and his little chest rising and falling with ease. It was a quiet act of care, one of many that marked their growing bond.

One afternoon, not long after switching to the harness, they took Rusty to the park. The sun was low, casting long shadows across the grass, and Rusty trotted ahead with a new kind of confidence. He wasn't straining anymore—just moving with purpose, ears perked, tail high. Sandy watched him closely, noticing how the harness seemed to cradle him rather than restrain him. It was more than a tool; it was a sign that they were learning about him, adapting to his needs, honoring his spirit. That walk felt different. Rusty wasn't just being walked—he was being understood.

The Gentle Observer with a Guarded Heart

Rusty earned a reputation at the park as the great kisser. He greeted nearly every dog with a lick on the nose or a playful nuzzle, his affection boundless and sincere. But not all dogs—or their humans—welcomed his enthusiastic displays of love. Still, Rusty didn't mind. He gave his kisses freely, as if joy were something to be shared.

At home, though, he was different.

Despite being playful with his parents—especially with Mom—Rusty was surprisingly evasive when it came to physical affection. He wasn't a lapdog. He preferred the comfort of his own bed in the family room, where he could rest and observe life unfolding around him. He felt the love in the house, and he knew he was cared for, but he kept a quiet distance, as if touch were something to be earned slowly.

Rusty was a fearful little soul. In his early days at home, he hesitated to cross the living room from the kitchen to Sandy's office. The threshold to the lanai felt like a boundary too wide. Open hands offering hugs made him flinch. On walks, he was wary of trash cans, parked cars, and garden figurines—each one a potential threat in his cautious mind.

But his fearfulness had a silver lining: it made him prudent. Rusty didn't rush into situations. He paused, assessed, and only moved when he felt safe. If Mom or Dad left the back door open, he wouldn't dart in or out. He'd wait for a clear signal, a quiet assurance that it was okay. He had seen the wind slam that lanai door before, and he didn't trust it. Ever watchful, he made sure not to get squashed, hesitating to go in unless he saw it secured in some way or held open for him.

Rusty's caution showed in the little things. When Mom and Dad were in the kitchen, he'd quietly retreat, choosing distance over curiosity. He didn't want to be stepped on or caught in the crossfire of a falling utensil. The clanking of pots and pans, the hiss of steam — it was all too much. He understood that this was their domain, especially during that sacred time of day when aromas filled the air and rhythms quickened. He didn't belong in the kitchen, and he knew it.

If Rusty were human, he probably wouldn't care much for cooking — or eating, for that matter. It just wasn't his thing. His appetite lived elsewhere: in play, in companionship, in the quiet corners of the house where love didn't clang or sizzle.

Still, Rusty wasn't entirely indifferent to food. He had his moments — peculiar, precise moments. Like when Dad peeled a banana. That soft snap of the skin, that faintly sweet scent drifting through the air — Rusty would appear, silent and expectant, as if summoned by some invisible signal. He didn't beg, exactly. He just stared, with that quiet intensity that made it hard to ignore him. Bananas were his exception. Not sizzling pans, not bubbling pots. Just the quiet fruit, peeled with care. It was as if he'd made a deal with the kitchen: no chaos, no clatter — just the occasional offering, delivered in peace.

Rusty offers kisses to other dogs

Sandra Haydee Giroux

Chapter Three

A Standoff in the Dark

One evening, Sandy took Rusty to the park to play with his usual buddies. As the sun dipped below the horizon—early January in Florida meant sunset came swiftly around 5:45—one by one, the other dogs and their humans left. Soon, it was just Sandy and Rusty. Normally, Rusty would not come easily to Mom when it was time to go home. Many times, she had to lure him with treats, or someone else would gently scoop him up for her.

This time, she called him over to hook on his leash and head home, but Rusty wouldn't come. He darted away from her outstretched hands, not in defiance, but in something deeper— something she could never quite name. Was it the leash he resisted? The feeling of being restrained? Whatever it was, it lived inside him like a quiet refusal.

As Sandy tried again and again to coax him, the light vanished completely. The park fell into pitch darkness. No moon, no streetlights—just shadows and silence. And still, Rusty ran. She could see in his eyes that he wasn't trying to escape her. He was wrestling with something within himself.

By 7:00 p.m., Sandy was still alone in the dark, unable to catch him and with no one around to help. She turned on her car's headlights and left the engine running, casting a weak glow across the field. Then she called Art, who was working the second shift and wouldn't be off until 8:00. She decided to wait.

What Sandy didn't know was that coyotes often lurked in the area after dark. The park, so familiar by day, had become a place of quiet danger.

Maybe Rusty sensed it, too. Maybe he was just tired. But the next time Sandy approached, he didn't run. He stayed where he was, still and silent, and let her take hold of him.

She kindly placed him on her chest, as he usually liked to be carried, his chin resting on her shoulder, embraced in the warmth and care that he so much needed.

After that night, something shifted. He never fully surrendered, but when other dogs left with their owners, Rusty began to cooperate—just a little. Enough to let Sandy know he was trying.

A Flight Risk

Another time at the dog park, Sandy and Rusty were alone, enjoying a quiet moment. A man approached with his own dog — a cute female, about Rusty's size — but instead of using the double-gated entrance like everyone else, he opted for the single-gated service entrance, the one reserved for lawn crews on Fridays.

The moment the gate creaked open, Rusty's instincts kicked in. He darted toward it like a bullet, his tiny body already halfway through the opening before Sandy could react.

"Nooooo!" she cried, her voice barely audible, stretched thin with panic. She reached out instinctively, arm extended, though Rusty was far beyond her grasp.

In a flash, the man stepped in — literally. He placed the upper part of his foot gently but firmly against Rusty's chest and nudged him back inside the park. Rusty tumbled to the ground in a swirl of fur and dust, startled but unharmed.

Sandy rushed over, heart pounding, knees weak. That was the moment she understood, without a doubt: Rusty was a flight risk.

On other occasions, Rusty would hurl himself off the moving golf cart while riding with either Mom or Dad. They learned to keep one foot hovering over the brake and one hand firmly on the leash, ready for his sudden leaps. Anything could lure him—fluttering leaves, distant squirrels, but especially female dogs passing by. His enthusiasm was boundless, and his timing unpredictable. More than once, they had to reel him back mid-air, hearts racing, grateful for the leash that kept him tethered to safety. Rusty didn't know danger; he only knew desire.

After each near escape, Art and Sandy would exchange glances—half exasperated, half amused. Rusty demanded constant vigilance, a readiness to act at any moment. It wasn't just about keeping him safe; it was about keeping up with him, matching his energy, anticipating his whims. They began to move differently, think differently—always with Rusty in mind. His presence reshaped their routines, their instincts, even their sense of time. Life with Rusty was unpredictable, but it was also vibrant. And in that vigilance, they discovered a new kind of attentiveness—not just to him, but to each other.

Sometimes, Sandy would daydream about taking a family trip to Pennsylvania, back to Rusty's previous home. She wondered if Rusty's heart had stayed behind in Pennsylvania, tucked between the pine trees and the scent of campfire. She wondered what he would do—would he light up with recognition? Would he run to them? Or would he choose to stay by her side? Deep down, she had her doubts. She loved him fiercely, but she wasn't always sure if he loved her back in the same way. Rusty was loyal, yes—but loyalty didn't always mean attachment. And in quiet moments, that uncertainty settled in like a shadow.

A New Look for Rusty

Time passed, and Rusty reached four months of age — time for his first haircut. Doodles don't shed, so without regular grooming, their hair grows endlessly into a mop of curls. That hypoallergenic trait was one of the reasons Art and Sandy chose the breed. Doodles are also known for their eagerness to please and quick-learning nature, making them relatively easy to train with positive reinforcement — though, of course, every dog has its own learning style and quirks.

When Sandy arrived at the groomer to pick Rusty up, she expected to see the familiar brownish hairball. But when she peered over the counter, she was met by a pair of lively, honeyed eyes gazing up at her. He looked like he was smiling. Sandy was stunned — her baby now resembled a growing pre-teen boy, taller and more mature than just a month before. When the groomer reached for the leash, Rusty gently declined, locking eyes with Sandy in silent request:

Pick me up. She understood instantly.

The Ride Home and Rusty's Signature Moves

He loved being carried like that — one paw hooked over her shoulder, the other resting on her chest, chin nestled against her neck, his back legs wrapped around her waist like a toddler clinging to his mother. Sandy placed him in his usual spot: the center flat piece between the two front seats of the car. That was his throne, and no one dared claim it. Before driving off, she paused to take him in. Rusty stretched his neck, scanning the world with curiosity, pretending not to notice his mom watching him. He was the great pretender, as Sandy liked to call him. In their backyard games, he'd tease her into chasing him — darting to one side of the yard, turning his head away while slyly watching her from the corner of his eye. Just when she got close enough to grab him, he'd bolt to the opposite side and repeat the trick, keeping her on the chase with gleeful mischief.

A Frightening First & `A Mother's Embrace

One quiet afternoon, Mom and Rusty found themselves alone in the small dog park. The sun was gentle, the breeze soft, and Rusty was happily trotting around, sniffing the grass and greeting the occasional squirrel. Then, a woman entered the park with a large, elegant white greyhound. Though the park was meant for small dogs, the greyhound seemed kind and graceful, and he began to run with effortless speed.

But in a split second, everything changed.

The greyhound's powerful stride swept too close, and before Rusty could react, he was knocked over. It wasn't aggressive—it was just a mismatch of size and speed—but for Rusty, it was terrifying. His world, once filled with trust and playfulness, suddenly felt unsafe.

Mom! Help me! he cried out in panic, his voice piercing the air.

Sandy saw it all. She bent down instantly, her voice calm but urgent:

"Rusty, come!"

In a flash, Rusty bolted toward her, his little legs pumping with fear. He dove into her arms, panting, trembling, and seeking the safety he knew only she could provide. She held him close, her embrace firm and reassuring, whispering comfort without words. In that moment, Rusty learned something new—not just about fear, but about love. His mom would always be there. No matter what.

Playing with Daddy

At home, Rusty and Daddy shared their own brand of joyful mayhem. Their playtime rituals were sacred — full of laughter, growls, and goofy theatrics. Daddy would drop to his knees and crawl on all fours, inviting Rusty into the game with exaggerated movements and mock-serious expressions. Rusty never hesitated. With a burst of excitement, he'd pounce, grabbing one of Daddy's limbs and letting out his signature growls — half fierce, half adorable.

I got you, Daddy! Surrender! he seemed to say, his eyes gleaming with mischief, pure, unfiltered joy.

Rusty's tail would wag like a metronome set to happiness. These moments, silly and sweet, became part of their daily rhythm — a language of love spoken in growls, giggles, and playful tackles.

Fastidious Boy!

No veggies, please!

Rusty's culinary preferences were as refined as they were stubborn. Breakfast was always a negotiation. Sandy would offer a turkey or chicken patty, gently placing it in front of him with hope in her eyes. Rusty, ever the critic, would sniff, then turn his little nose from side to side — a polite but firm refusal. He'd rather skip breakfast entirely than compromise his standards.

During the day, however, he was a different dog. At the park, he'd accept training treats with enthusiasm, fueled by the thrill of play and the joy of companionship. He'd run, leap, and chase with boundless energy, as if powered by pure will.

But come dinnertime, Rusty transformed into a ravenous gourmet. His appetite surged, but his standards remained. Meat was non-negotiable. Kibbles were tolerated — barely. Sandy, ever hopeful, tried sneaking in fresh vegetables, finely chopped and mixed with his meat. Rusty would sniff them out like a truffle hunter, delicately picking around the intruders and leaving a neat pile of rejected greens. Fruit? Absolutely not. That was a line he wouldn't cross.

And then there was the ritual: he would only eat from Sandy's hand. No bowl, no plate — just the familiar warmth of her palm. It wasn't just about food. It was about trust, comfort, and a little dash of drama. Rusty was a fastidious boy, and Sandy wouldn't have him any other way.

Park Friends

The dog park was Rusty's kingdom — a place of freedom, friendship, and mischievous delight. One of his favorite games with Sandy began with a signature move: he'd trot over, spread his front legs wide, lower his chest to the ground, and let out a playful growl. His eyes sparkled with challenge.

Get me if you can, Mom!

And when Sandy lunged to catch him, he'd dart around her with lightning speed, zero in on her sneakers, and — with surgical precision — undo the laces. Then came the triumphant laugh, loud and proud, as if he'd just outwitted the world.

Rusty had a vibrant social circle. Lily, the high-energy whirlwind, was his match in speed and spirit. They'd chase each other in dizzying loops, switching roles with joyful abandon. Bella adored him, spinning in giddy circles just to catch his eye. Luna and Daisy joined the fun, but Rusty favored Luna — she knew how to play the chase game just right, letting him feel like the hero in pursuit.

Among the boys, he had a select crew: Max the fluffy Pomeranian, Milo the scrappy mutt, Rhin the elegant Sheltie, and Charlie the bold Chihuahua. They shared his zest for play, though most male dogs preferred to keep their distance. Rusty didn't mind. He'd still greet them with kisses, undeterred by growls or cold shoulders — love was his default setting.

And then there were the Dachshunds, Zoey and Cooper — a trio of adorableness when together. Rusty moved through the park like a diplomat and a jester, winning hearts, dodging feet, and making every visit feel like a celebration.

I GOT YOU,
DADDY!
SURRENDER!

- Fun at the park
- Rusty's first haircut, "the great pretender."

Sandra Haydee Giroux

Chapter Four

Park Chatter

The sun was dipping low, casting golden light across the dog park as Rusty zipped past a cluster of chatting owners.

Lily's mom (laughing): "There he goes again — shoelace bandit on the loose!"

Sandy (grinning): "He thinks it's a tactical win. I'm just glad he hasn't figured out Velcro."

Bella's owner: "He's got charm, that one. Bella spins like a top every time she sees him."

Sandy: "He's a little heartbreaker. I swear he flirts."

Luna's dad: "He and Luna are perfect together. She loves being chased, and he loves the chase. It's like watching a rom-com in fast-forward."

Max's owner: "Rusty's got diplomacy too. Max usually growls at anyone who gets too close, but Rusty just kisses him and walks away like nothing happened."

Sandy: "He doesn't take it personally. He's all about peace treaties and playtime."

Charlie's owner: "I've never seen a dog with such expressive eyes. He looks like he's planning something — and then he *does*."

Sandy: "Oh, he's always scheming. Especially if it involves treats or shoelaces."

Zoey and Cooper's owner: "I love when they all sit together like a little council of cuteness. It's like they're plotting world domination — or snack time."

Sandy (softly): "He brings out the best in everyone. Even the grumpy ones."

The group chuckled, watching Rusty dart through the grass, tail high, heart open. In that moment, he wasn't just Sandy's dog — he was everyone's joy.

Best Friends Forever

At five months old, Rusty had reached his full height — lanky, confident, and bursting with energy. One golden afternoon at the park, fate intervened. A dark chocolate mini-Labradoodle with mesmerizing green eyes strolled by with her mom. Her name was Dixie.

Rusty spotted her instantly. He barked — not just any bark, but an inviting, melodic call that said, *come play with me.* Dixie paused, tilted her head, and wagged her tail. She understood. Within moments, she was inside the park, and the two were off — running, wrestling, tumbling through the grass like old friends reunited.

It was love at first sight. Not romantic, but something deeper — a soul-level recognition. Rusty, with his rebellious streak and happy-go-lucky charm, had met his match. Dixie mirrored his spirit, and together they moved like dancers choreographed by joy. They ran side by side, perfectly synchronized, taking turns chasing and being chased. Their energy was boundless, their laughter — yes, laughter—contagious.

Rusty would lie on his back, paws in the air, and Dixie would hover above him, playfully nudging and teasing. It was a game only they understood, a language of movement and mirth. From that day forward, they met every evening at the park. Rain, cold, heat — nothing stopped them. Their moms, devoted and smiling, made sure the playdate happened, no matter the season.

Winter melted into spring, spring bloomed into summer, and fall painted the trees with gold. Through it all, Rusty and Dixie lived their greatest adventure — almost a year of pure friendship. And each night, Rusty slept soundly, dreaming of green eyes and grassy fields, knowing that tomorrow would bring another dance, another chase, another moment with his best friend.

Bilingual Boy

Rusty wasn't just smart — he was multilingual. Without any formal exposure to Spanish, he somehow understood it, as if the language had seeped into his soul through love and repetition. Sandy, of Hispanic heritage, often spoke to him in Spanish, and he responded with uncanny precision. "Date la vuelta," she'd say — "Turn around" — and he'd spin in place like a dancer hitting his mark. "Ya regreso," she'd whisper — "I'll be back" — and he'd wait patiently, eyes fixed on the door, trusting her return.

One afternoon, Sandy and Rusty visited Grandma. Sandy sat on the couch with Rusty curled beside her, while Grandma relaxed in her favorite loveseat. With a gentle smile, Grandma called out in Spanish, "Ven aquí, a mi lado" — "Come over here, by me." Rusty didn't hesitate. He hopped down and trotted over to Grandma's side, settling in with quiet pride.

It became a ritual. After playtime at the park, as the sun dipped low and the sky turned golden, Sandy would call out, "Ok, vamos a la casa, Rusty!"— "Ok, let's go home, Rusty!"

At the sound of her voice, Rusty would drop his front paws to the ground, tail wagging wildly, eyes gleaming with mischief. With a sharp bark, he'd seem to tell Dixie,

Mom's calling me home, Dixie! One more round before we go!

And off they'd go again—chasing, wrestling, nipping at each other's legs, their joy echoing through the fading light.

Sandy watched in awe. It was as if Rusty had always known the language, as if love had taught him the meaning behind the words. She was reminded of how children absorb language—not through grammar drills, but through connection, tone, and trust. Rusty was her bilingual boy—intuitive, attuned, and always ready to understand the heart behind the voice.

As the last rays of sunlight stretched across the grass, Rusty finally slowed down, his energy spent, his joy lingering in the air like laughter. Dixie trotted beside him, their play winding down into quiet companionship. Sandy clipped on his leash and began the walk back to the golf cart, her heart full. The park was nearly empty now, the world settling into evening. Rusty glanced up at her once, his eyes warm and knowing, and in that moment, she felt it—not just the bond, but the trust. The kind that doesn't need words. The kind that says, *I'm yours.*

Open Defiance

It was a quiet weekend afternoon at the park — no dogs, no Dixie, just Sandy and Rusty. The air was still, and Rusty wasn't interested in squirrels or fetch. He wanted company, not solitude. Sandy sat under the shelter on a bench, watching as Rusty wandered off and found a ball to chew. Then, he discovered a ball launcher with a long handle — a new treasure. He grabbed it and began gnawing with gusto.

Half an hour passed. Sandy stood up, ready to go.

"Time to go home, Rusty. Let's go."

Rusty didn't even look up. *Chew chew chew.* His response was clear:

Nope.

"Rusty! Let's go!"

Nope.

Sandy raised an eyebrow. "Ah, no? Okay, I'm going home."

OK.

She walked toward the exit, passing through the two gated section that formed a protective buffer. She left the first gate open — the one leading from the small dog park where Rusty sat, still chewing. Then she locked the second gate behind her and walked around the perimeter. No one was around. Rusty kept chewing, undisturbed.

Sandy reached the golf cart, turned the key, backed up, and began to drive away — just six feet or so.

Suddenly, Rusty dropped the launcher. His ears perked. He ran to the chain-link fence, paws up, eyes wide.

Mom! Mom! Wait! MOM!

He barked with urgency, desperation in every sound. His eyes followed her, pleading. Sandy turned and looked back. His bark pierced her heart — raw, panicked, full of regret.

She stepped off the cart and walked toward him. Rusty bolted to the open gate, then waited at the second one, tail low, eyes apologetic. Sandy quietly lifted him into her arms and carried him to the cart.

Sorry, Mom. And thanks for being patient with me.

From that day forward, Rusty never hesitated when Sandy called. The lesson had landed — not through punishment, but through love, trust, and a moment of heartbreak that neither of them would forget.

Lessons in Love and Leashes

After that unsettling time at the park, Art and Sandy sat down to talk. Rusty's behavior had raised concerns—not just about safety, but about his emotional well-being. They agreed: it was time for obedience training.

Rusty enrolled in a seven-week program, learning commands alongside other dogs. He was the youngest and the smallest. To everyone's surprise, he thrived. He loved practicing in the park with Art and Sandy, especially when treats were involved. He took the commands seriously, responding with precision and focus. Sit. Stay. Heel. Rusty wasn't just learning—he was evolving.

During one class, Sandy was walking Rusty in a group exercise when Rusty spotted Art sitting nearby, gently caressing a beautiful standard Poodle belonging to the trainer. Rusty's ears perked up. His eyes locked onto the scene. He was distracted, visibly unsettled.

When the walk ended and Rusty approached Art, he let out a loud, unmistakable growl at the Poodle. It was clear: Rusty was jealous.

That's my dad, you Poodle!

Funny thing is, Rusty himself was half Poodle — but heritage wasn't exactly on his mind at that moment.

Sandy couldn't help but smile. It was the first time Rusty had shown such a possessive affection.

Actually, that's a good sign, she thought. *He's showing his love for Daddy – he really cares!*

Later that evening, Rusty curled up in his bed by Daddy, still brooding over the Poodle incident.

"You know," Daddy said, scratching behind his ears, "Rusty's got a little Poodle in him too."

Rusty's ears perked up.

Poodle? Me?

He glanced at his reflection in the sliding glass door — the curls, the alert eyes, the proud stance.

Maybe that Poodle wasn't so different after all.

But he still didn't like how that dog wagged his tail at Daddy.

At the end of the course, Rusty graduated from kindergarten training with pride. He received a certificate, and a photo was taken to mark the occasion. That training didn't just teach him obedience—it helped him mature. It became part of who he was.

Sandra Haydee Giroux

Rusty's Graduation Speech

(As imagined by Sandy, translated from tail wags and happy barks)

"Thank you, everyone — especially Mom and Dad — for believing in me, even when I was more fluff than focus. I've learned a lot these past seven weeks: how to sit, stay, heel... and how not to growl at Poodles who flirt with my dad. (Still working on that one.)

To my classmates: you were bigger, louder, and sometimes faster — but I kept up, and I'm proud of that. To my trainers: thanks for the treats. I mean, the wisdom. Mostly the treats.

And to Dixie — my best friend, my chase partner, my shoelace witness — I promise to keep practicing so I can impress her at the park.

I may be small, but my heart is huge. I'm ready for the next adventure — with love, loyalty, and just a little bit of drama.

Signed,
🐾 Rusty
Certified Good Boy

A Quiet Reflection

As the dogs played and the sun began its slow descent, Sandy found herself sitting beside Bella's owner, Maria — a quiet woman with kind eyes and a soft voice. Rusty had just finished a round of chase and was now lying at Sandy's feet, panting happily.

Maria (gazing at Rusty): "You know... he came to me once. I was sitting right over there, crying. I didn't think anyone noticed."
Sandy (surprised): "Rusty did?"
Maria: "Yes. I'd just lost my sister. I didn't want to talk to anyone. But Rusty walked right up, sat beside me, and leaned his head against my leg. No barking, no fuss. Just... presence."
Sandy (softly): "He's always known when someone needs comfort."
Maria: "I didn't even know his name then. But I remember thinking, *this dog understands.* I cried into his fur for a few

minutes. He didn't move. Just stayed with me."

Sandy: "He's done that with me too. Especially when I couldn't speak much. He just listened."

Maria (smiling): "He's more than a dog. He's a soul with fur."

Rusty stirred, then looked up at Maria and gave her a gentle lick on the hand — as if to say, *I remember.* The moment passed quietly, but it lingered in the air like a soft echo. Around them, the park buzzed with laughter and barking, but in that small corner, there was peace.

Chapter Five

An Emergency

At that particular time in their lives, Art and Sandy shared just one car — the one Sandy used for her daily commute. Art stayed home, relying on their golf cart for short trips around the neighborhood.

One quiet afternoon, Art was sitting in the backyard, watching Rusty roam and sniff through the grass. Two oak trees stood like sentinels on the property, their roots tangled beneath the soil, while a few stubborn bushes lined the fence. Rusty moved with his usual curiosity, nose to the ground, tail swaying gently.

Then, suddenly, he froze.

He began pawing at his snout in frantic desperation, twisting and jerking as if trying to claw something out. Art's heart dropped. Rusty was choking — or so it seemed. Maybe a stick, maybe some object lodged in his throat.

Art didn't hesitate. He scooped Rusty into his arms and ran to the nearest neighbor's house, pounding on the door. No answer.

Still clutching the trembling creature, he sprinted to another house. This time, a woman opened the door. She took one look at Rusty and sprang into action.

"I'll drive," she said, already grabbing her keys. She turned to her husband, who was ill and resting inside. "Don't move. Don't go anywhere. I'll be right back."

They sped off, Art holding Rusty close as the dog writhed in discomfort, his movements growing more desperate. Art tried to soothe him, but fear gripped his chest.

At the vet's office, time blurred.

Finally, the diagnosis: a cracked acorn had wedged itself between Rusty's back teeth.

A simple fix.

A massive scare.

Later that evening, the house was still. The sun had dipped below the horizon, casting long shadows across the living room. Art sat on his armchair, Rusty curled in his bed beside him, his breathing steady now, his body relaxed.

The vet had said it was nothing serious — a cracked acorn, easily removed. But Art couldn't shake the image of Rusty pawing at his face, the panic in his eyes, the helplessness in his own chest.
He reached down and gently stroked Rusty's fur.

"You scared me today, buddy," he whispered.

Rusty didn't respond, of course. But he shifted closer, resting his chin on Art's armchair's footrest, as if to say, *I'm here. I'm okay.*

Art leaned back, letting the silence wrap around them. No clanking kitchen sounds, no rushing engines — just the soft hum of the evening and the warmth of a creature who, without words, had become part of his heart.
It was strange, Art thought, how quickly love could grow, how a dog could become family. How a cracked acorn could remind you of everything that mattered.

A Middle Name for Rusty

The babies were tumbling in the grass, giggling and chasing bubbles, while their moms sat nearby on the park bench, sipping iced coffees and swapping stories.

"I just realized," said Marlene, adjusting her sunglasses, "we never talked about our pets' middle names."

"Middle names?" laughed Tanya. "You mean like… official ones? Or the ones we yell when they're in trouble?"

"Both count," Marlene grinned. "Okay, I'll go first. My cat's full name is Muffin Louise. Don't ask why — she just looks like a Louise."

Tanya chimed in. "Mine's Bruno James. It sounds dignified, like he's a retired boxer who now teaches yoga."

They turned to Sandy, who smiled, already knowing what she'd say.

"Rusty Papito," she said proudly.

"Papito?" Tanya raised an eyebrow. "What kind of name is that?"

Sandy chuckled. "It's a word of endearment in my culture. In Spanish, we use it for dads, sons, boyfriends, even elderly men we love. It's affectionate — warm. At home, that's what I call him. Papito."

The other two nodded, intrigued.

"That's actually really sweet," Marlene said. "Rusty Papito. Sounds like a little prince."

Sandy looked out at Rusty, who was sniffing a patch of grass with great purpose. "He is," she said softly. "In his own way."

Just then, Rusty trotted over with a stick twice his size, tail wagging in excitement. He dropped it at Sandy's feet and barked once — sharp and proud.

"Papito!" Sandy laughed. "You're showing off now?"

Marlene leaned forward. "He knows we're talking about him. That bark had attitude."

Tanya giggled. "If I called my husband 'Papito,' he'd probably ask if I wanted something."

Marlene nodded. "I like that. It sounds sweet. Maybe I'll try it with my dog. He's been ignoring me lately — maybe he just wants a fancy nickname."

The three ladies laughed, the kind of laughter that feels warm and familiar.

Rusty curled up beside Sandy, resting his chin on her shoe.

"He's been so many things to me," Sandy said softly. "A friend, a helper, someone who always listens. Papito fits."

The Ice Cream Party and Al's Arrival

Sandy's days of working from home had quietly come to an end. The rhythm of remote work, once a gentle balm during her recovery, gave way to the bustle of full-time hours in town. Her evenings were now condensed into a single visit to the park — a brief but cherished window of time with Rusty.

When Rusty turned one, Sandy marked the milestone with a celebration that felt more like a neighborhood festival than a simple doggy birthday. She brought doggy ice cream — the kind that melted slowly and smelled faintly of peanut butter — and handed it out to the doodles and mutts who had become Rusty's regular playmates. Rusty, tail high and eyes gleaming, raced around the park like he was hosting the event himself. The other dogs chased him in joyful chaos, their paws kicking up little clouds of dust in the fading light.

It was during this season of transition that Al arrived.

A cousin of Art's, Al came to stay while he searched for work. He was young, easygoing, and had a natural way with animals. Rusty took to him immediately — no hesitation, no warm-up period. From the first day, it was as if they'd known each other for years.

Al became Rusty's evening companion, taking him to the park without fail. He didn't just walk Rusty — he played with him, talked to him, introduced him to new dogs, and made sure he never missed a moment of social joy. Sandy, watching from the sidelines when she could, felt a quiet gratitude. Al's presence filled the gap her new schedule had created.

The park became their stage. Al and Rusty, a duo of charm and energy, drew smiles from strangers and made fast friends. Rusty's confidence bloomed. Al's laughter echoed across the field. For five months, they were inseparable — two spirits finding joy in the simple act of showing up, every single day.

Sandy's Quiet Reflection

Some evenings, Sandy would arrive at the park just in time to catch the tail end of Rusty's playtime. She'd spot him from a distance — a blur of golden curls darting between dogs, Al jogging behind with a grin that matched Rusty's energy. It was a lovely sight. And it stung, just a little.

She sat on the bench, the one near the oak tree where the breeze always seemed to linger. Watching them, she felt a mix of pride and ache. Rusty was thriving. He was social, confident, joyful. Al had become his buddy, his daily anchor. And Sandy — well, she was now the observer.

It wasn't jealousy. It was something quieter. A soft mourning for the days when she was the one Rusty waited for at the door, eyes wide with anticipation. Now, he waited for Al. And Sandy understood. Life had shifted. Rusty was growing, and so was she.

She smiled as Al tossed a ball and Rusty bounded after it, ears flapping like wings. This was what she had hoped for — a happy, well-loved dog with a full life. Still, as the sun dipped below the trees and the park began to empty, Sandy felt the tug of something tender.

She walked over, knelt beside Rusty, and scratched behind his ears. He leaned into her, just for a moment, and she whispered, "I missed you today." Rusty licked her cheek in reply, and that was enough.

By then, Rusty had long outgrown the baby hold. His once-rust-colored fur had lightened, bleached by sun and time, now closer to blond than bronze. Only the brown spots around his nose and eyes remained. His name no longer matched his appearance—but it still fit where it mattered. He was Rusty at heart.

Names, she thought, don't always describe. Sometimes they just remember.

Chapter Six

No more Dixie

By the time Rusty turned one and reached his full fifteen pounds, Dixie had begun having stomach problems. Her parents took her to the vet several times, hoping for answers. The vet suspected she might be picking up something harmful at the dog park and recommended she stay away — for her own good. It was the right decision for Dixie. But for Rusty, it was a heartbreak.

He didn't understand the change. He only knew that his routine had shifted — that the joyful rhythm of playtime, followed by peaceful sleep, had been interrupted. Sandy and Art still took him to the park faithfully, but Dixie was no longer there.

That particular afternoon, Sandy and Rusty were alone. Rusty sat quietly, chewing on toys he found scattered in the grass. Every so often, he lifted his head toward the path where Dixie usually arrived. Nothing. He resumed chewing, then wandered the park, searching for something — anything — to spark joy.

He paused again, this time facing the parking lot. Maybe she'd come in her golf cart, her mom beside her. But the space remained empty.

No Dixie.

Not that day.

Not the next.

Not the one after.

Rusty couldn't make sense of it. His playmate had vanished, and the world felt dimmer. Sandy saw it in his posture — slower walks, heavier steps, eyes that seemed to carry weight. His sadness was quiet but unmistakable.

At home, he began climbing onto the couch, perching his chin on the armrest, staring out the window that faced the backyard. He didn't bark. He didn't whine. He just watched, as if waiting for something he couldn't name.

Sandy felt his loneliness like a thread tugging at her heart. She wished she could explain, or fix it, or bring Dixie back. But all she could do was sit nearby, offering quiet companionship.

Time passed. Five months of slow healing. Rusty began playing with other dogs again, but it was clear — the spark wasn't the same. Dixie had been more than a playmate. She had been his joy.

Her absence left a silence in Rusty's days, a space where laughter used to live.

Far from the quiet ache of Rusty's days, in a country town nestled among Pennsylvania hills, life stirred gently.
A mini Golden Doodle, warm and watchful, curled around seven newborn puppies — three boys and four girls, each one a golden spark.
They didn't know it yet, but one of them was destined for a boy with heavy eyes and a heart still waiting to heal.
The world, in its quiet wisdom, was already stitching joy back into place.

A New Family Member

Two months later, Sandy shared with Art her desire to bring home a second doodle—a companion for Rusty. At first, Art resisted. The idea felt premature, maybe even impractical. But as days passed, he found himself reflecting on it. Quiet moments turned into quiet searches, and one evening, while browsing online, he saw her.

A beautiful mini Golden Doodle, just two months old. Her name was Jewel.

They had looked locally, but nothing felt right. Jewel, however, stayed on his mind. Art kept checking the website, watching her listing week after week. She was still available. And with each passing day, his heart leaned further toward her. There was something in her eyes—wide, wondering, full of softness—that tugged at him.

He showed Sandy. She agreed: Jewel was adorable. Maybe she was the one.

Art began talking to Rusty about her. Sitting on the couch, he'd stroke Rusty's fur and speak gently, telling him about the little sister who might soon arrive. "You'll have so much fun," he'd say. Rusty would tilt his head, listening intently, trying to understand Daddy's kind words. Words that carried a promise. A plan. A change.

Art noticed the price for Jewel was dropping. She had two things that made others hesitate: she wasn't housebroken, and she had an abdominal hernia. By now, she was five months old. Still waiting.

Then, one day, her listing disappeared.

Someone had purchased her.

And that someone… was Art.

He had made his decision. The arrangements were finalized. Payment and vaccine paperwork exchanged remotely. Jewel was coming home.

Will This Plan Work?

Sandy shared her concerns with Al over coffee one morning.

"What do you think, Al? Would Rusty accept a little sister after all this time being the only dog?"

Al smiled thoughtfully. "I think, as long as you two keep showing him he's the alpha dog, he'll be fine. He just needs to feel the same affection you'll give her. He'll know she's a puppy."

This time, they chose ground transportation to bring her home. They had a new name ready, one that felt just right. The deal was sealed.

And as fate would have it, she arrived on the Fourth of July (Independence Day in the U.S.).

She came home with fireworks in the sky and excitement in the air—because she was a little hurricane.

After a two-day journey, the transport team finally arrived. When they knocked on the door, they held her gently in their arms. She was trembling like a leaf in the fall, her tail tucked tightly between her legs. She had never had a haircut, and her coat had grown wild and woolly—five inches of golden fluff that made her look like a walking cotton ball.

Heidi's First Day at Home

Art and Sandy had arranged for Rusty and Heidi to meet in the backyard. Though Heidi had been trembling when she was delivered, the moment she saw Rusty—handsome, poised, and just her size—it was love at first sight. She knew. This was her family.

With a burst of joy, they began to run side by side across the yard. Her long, golden hair rippled like waves behind her. She had a playful quirk when she ran—leaping over Rusty mid-stride, a move she'd later repeat with other dogs. Her eyes were barely visible beneath her fluffy coat, and her grooming appointment was already set for the next day.

Heidi was bubbly, bold, and brimming with excitement. Every time Mom or Dad returned—even if they'd only been gone ten minutes—she greeted them as if they'd been away for days. Her joy reset with every reunion.

That night, as Sandy and Art settled into their armchairs, Heidi made her move. Without hesitation, she jumped onto Daddy's footrest and curled up by his feet, claiming her spot with quiet confidence.

Rusty watched, stunned.

That stranger just curled up by Daddy's feet?

He had never dared to jump into Daddy's chair, never nestled so close. He approached the armrest and gave it a gentle nose-butt—his way of asking permission. Art understood and invited him up. Soon, both dogs were curled by his feet.

But Rusty wasn't at ease.

He was no longer the only baby in the house. Was she staying for the night? Forever? So, he decided to take matters into his own paws.

Take her back, Daddy! he barked.

"She's part of the family now, Rusty," Art said gently. "She's your little sister."

Rusty's instincts flared. This newcomer was a threat to his place, his people. When Heidi hopped off the chair, Rusty followed—and lunged. He growled and pinned her down,

fierce but controlled. He didn't bite; he didn't want to hurt her. He just needed to be heard.

Sandy gasped, concerned.

"Ah ha ha! They need this," Art said calmly. "They'll be fine."

And Heidi? She knew exactly what to do. She lay on her back, submissive and still, accepting Rusty's roar without resistance. Even when his teeth gently gripped her nose, she remained undamaged—physically and emotionally.

Rusty released his frustration. The storm passed.

She had passed the test.

And from that moment on, he accepted her.

Sandy learned something that night. Rusty's growl wasn't just a protest—it was proof. Proof that he belonged, that he cared deeply for his home, his territory, and the love of Mom and Dad. From that moment on, she never again wondered about that family trip to Pennsylvania. She no longer needed to test where Rusty's heart was. She knew.

A New Heidi

The next day, July 5th, Art and Sandy took hairy Heidi to the groomer. The groomer suggested they snap a before-and-after photo—and they did. When they returned to pick her up, they could hardly believe the transformation. Heidi was radiant. Her big, floppy ears framed her face with a girlish charm, and her golden coat shimmered with softness. She looked like a brand-new pup.

As Sandy brought her to the car, Rusty—waiting inside with Al—watched intently. His eyes followed her every step as she approached. When she climbed in, he couldn't contain his excitement. He sniffed her all over, tail wagging.

Hmmm. She smells and looks good. I wish I could keep her...

Heidi didn't need a mirror to know she was loved. She felt it in the way they looked at her, spoke to her, welcomed her.

Later, on their walk around the neighborhood, Heidi resisted the leash at first—hopping, pulling, unsure of the rhythm. But then she looked at Rusty, walking calmly beside Art, and decided to follow his lead. Her steps grew more elegant, her head perked with pride, her glamorous tail always curled upward like a bouquet of plumes. She was learning.

Back at the house, her energy exploded. She launched into zoomies—darting from the bed to the sofa, from one couch to another, leaping high, sprinting fast, bounding from the lanai to the living room and back again. Her athleticism was undeniable. Art and Sandy knew she'd thrive with agility exercises.

Rusty watched in exhilarated ecstasy. Her wild joy stirred something in him. He growled playfully, jumped in, and together they wrestled, chased, and nipped at each other's legs in a dance of pure delight.

But Rusty also had his quiet moments. He'd retreat to his favorite corner of the couch, needing space. Heidi, intuitive and observant, followed his patterns—learning when to play and when to pause.

Heidi had to go through crate training too—at night and during set times each day. She barked loudly, her front paws scrabbling in rapid protest, making quite the commotion. Rusty watched her midday meltdown from right outside the crate. She seemed to be yelling:

"Let me out, let me out of here!"

Rusty just shook his head.

Sorry, I can't help you, girl, he seemed to say, and walked off to his couch.

That night, on her second day, Heidi approached Sandy as she rested in her armchair. She lifted her upper body and placed her front legs gently on the footrest, content just to be near Mom. Rusty came over and growled, a quiet correction for her boldness. But Heidi looked down at him, calm and unbothered, and softly placed one paw over his face—as if to say:

"Chill out, buddy. I'm just keeping Mom company."

She was a witty and sassy girl.

Hmmmm. I actually like that, Rusty seemed to think, lowering his guard.

He was being trained by a puppy.

'You'll have so much fun.'
Rusty tilted his head as
he listened carefully.

A New Heidi

BEFORE   AFTER

1. Rusty waits for Dixie every day.
2. Rusty sits on his sofa staring at the backyard, longing to see her again.
3. Daddy talks to Rusty about his new sister. Rusty seems to imagine how she will be. (AI-generated picture)
4. Heidi on the 4th of July, then the next day. (AI-generated picture)
5. The real Heidi a day after her arrival.

Sandra Haydee Giroux

Chapter Seven

Departure

On the third day of Heidi's arrival, Al left for another city to pursue a new job. It was a bittersweet goodbye. Al was more than a relative—he was like a brother to Art and Sandy, and a buddy to Rusty. His absence left a quiet ache. Even the park friends asked for him. Everyone would miss him.

The house felt quieter after Al left. Rusty wandered from room to room, sniffing the corners where Al used to sit, pausing by the door as if waiting for it to open. He didn't bark or whine—just waited. His eyes held a question no one could answer.

Sandy noticed the shift. Rusty's tail didn't wag as much, and his playful growls were fewer. Even Heidi, in all her puppy exuberance, seemed to sense it. She followed him gently, not to play, but to be near. She curled beside him on the couch, her head resting on his back, her breath slow and steady.

Rusty didn't move.

But he didn't move away either.

It was the first time she'd comforted him—not with energy, but with presence. And in that quiet moment, something passed between them. Not words, not play—just understanding.

Heidi Reshapes Rusty's World

At first, Rusty merely tolerated his little thrilling sister. She was loud, impulsive, and had no sense of boundaries. But after a week of constant antics and unexpected joy, something shifted. Rusty realized he was having fun—real fun. The kind that made his tail wag without thinking. Still, love didn't come all at once. It crept in slowly, like sunlight warming a cold room. Sharing was hard. Sharing space, toys, attention, even food—it was a lot.

Heidi, for her part, was a handful. She had no training, no manners, and no shame. She inhaled her food like a vacuum, then burped and passed gas with theatrical flair. There was no food she would not eat. She'd steal bites from Mom's or Dad's plate if they weren't vigilant, and she had a sneaky habit of climbing onto dining chairs to snatch napkins, which she'd chew with suspicious quietness in the living room—always caught just in time.

Her body was longer than Rusty's, giving her the advantage of reaching the kitchen counter. She'd prop her front paws up and peer over with curiosity, never grabbing, just watching. Mom indulged her, letting her observe the meal prep like a tiny sous-chef. If Heidi were human, she'd be a home cook—the kitchen her sanctuary, her appetite insatiable.

This insatiability, oddly enough, became a blessing. Rusty, who had always been a reluctant eater, suddenly found himself in competition. Heidi would polish off her bowl and then eye his leftovers with shameless intent.

I refuse to let her eat my food. She has to be content with what she has, Rusty thought, indignantly.

And just like that, Rusty began eating with gusto. Vegetables, fruits, mixed greens, carrots—he devoured them all. Twice a day, without fail. He even started anticipating mealtime with the same excitement as Heidi.

When Sandy was preparing their meals, and Heidi was watching, she knew exactly when it was about time for the bowls to be set down. She'd start jumping in excitement, her whole body a spring of joy. At this signal, Rusty—who had to watch everything from below, or better yet, watch Heidi's reactions—also knew the moment was near. He'd begin nose-butting Sandy, urging her to hurry up.

Heidi's joy was contagious. Her rhythms became his rhythms. Her signals became his cues.

She was reshaping his world.

"Wow! This is a new Rusty!" Sandy exclaimed, thrilled. "When in his short life did he ever ask for food or eat broccoli? I'm over the moon!" And just like that, the days of hand-feeding Rusty were over.

Wherever Rusty walked, Heidi followed. To and from the backyard, side by side. On walks, they moved in tandem, hauling Sandy or Art like a pair of sled dogs. They were like twins yoked together—inseparable, though not without exceptions.

Rusty loved her. The whole family did. Despite her bad manners and the temporary chaos she brought—relieving herself wherever she pleased—Heidi was extremely sweet. When Rusty was being caressed, she'd join in, nudging for her share of affection.

At other times, when Rusty was about to receive a caress, Heidi would spot the moment and launch herself between him and Mom—catching her hand mid-air to steal the touch before it reached him. For Heidi, being caressed was top priority. It was doggy heaven, and she wasn't about to miss her turn. Rusty, ever the gentleman, would simply blink and sigh, as if to say,

Here we go again. He never growled at this or pushed back—he just let her have it.

She was a lap dog through and through, always seeking closeness.

Rusty learned that he was still the alpha. Heidi wasn't a threat—she was a complement. A needed one. She filled the spaces he didn't know were empty.

Play Time

Heidi was reckless, loud, and proudly self-appointed as the watchdog of the house. She'd perch atop the sofa facing the main door, barking at every sound, shadow, or imagined threat. Rusty, who had rarely barked before, and not to be outdone, became a ferocious barker himself. If she could bark like that, he had to bark louder and longer—since he was the alpha.

On walks, Heidi barked at every neighbor, every vehicle, every dog they passed. She wasn't familiar with this new world, and her defensiveness extended to herself and her loved ones. She had no fear of anything. Sandy watched with growing concern.

Under Heidi's influence, Rusty didn't just become an overprotective, loud barker—he also became a cuddler. Once Heidi was welcomed into Mom and Dad's bed alongside Rusty, he learned to snuggle, taking turns curling up against Dad, then switching to Mom's side to soak in their warmth. Heidi, ever the sentinel, preferred to lie by their feet, as if guarding the family while still showing affection and bonding.

It's said that people who cuddle with their dogs enjoy the release of endorphins—which reduces stress, lifts their mood, and eases pain. Rusty and Heidi gave all that, and more.

As time passed, Heidi grew taller and a pound or two heavier. Mom kept a close eye on her dinner portions to maintain a balanced diet; Heidi's puppy energy remained exuberant. She'd pull every toy from Rusty's basket, scattering them across the house without a thought of putting them back.

Daddy bought flavored toy bones for them to chew on. Even though they each had one, they always wanted the same one. So they learned to take turns. Heidi would chew first, then pass it off when she tired. But sometimes, Rusty outsmarted her.

One afternoon, Sandy was reading in the loveseat with Rusty curled beside her. Heidi was on the couch, chewing a toy bone with intense focus. Rusty watched her, then quietly got down, picked up the other bone, and placed it in the middle of the couch. He jumped off and waited. Heidi spotted it, paused for two seconds, then gave in to temptation. She dropped her bone, crossed to the other side of the couch, and began chewing the new one. Rusty climbed back up and reclaimed the first bone. And there they were—each happily chewing away, content in their clever little exchange.

Athletic Feat

One evening, Sandy was driving Rusty and Heidi to the park when a pair of blackbirds stood on the grass by the roadside. Heidi, who could never contain herself around birds or squirrels, launched herself off the moving golf cart and hit the ground in her attempt to run after the birds. But Sandy had one foot hovering over the brake and both leashes in hand. She slammed the brake and reeled Heidi back in before she could dart into the street.

Rusty, meanwhile, didn't even flinch. He'd long outgrown those impulsive feats and sat calmly, as if he'd seen it all before.

After that heart-pounding moment, Sandy decided not to take any more chances. She lowered the plastic side panel—the rain protector—on their side of the cart. It was the height of Florida summer, and the heat was stifling. But even though they were hot... they were also safe.

The daredevil squirrel

Sandy preferred taking Rusty and Heidi to the park during quieter hours—when few people or dogs were around—so Heidi could gradually acclimate to the environment. She devoted time to play with them, and Heidi quickly learned to fetch with Mom. But what thrilled her even more were the squirrels, especially one mischievous daredevil who loved to tease dogs.

The small dog park had two oak trees, one on each side, casting generous shade. It was the squirrel's home, and that particular squirrel—whom we'll call Chiney—had a flair for drama. Whenever Rusty and Heidi arrived, Chiney would dash from one tree to the other, triggering a wild chase. The three of them—two dogs and one squirrel—would race across the park in a game that Chiney seemed to relish.

One day, Heidi caught up to Chiney just as she reached the base of her tree—and this time, she actually caught her. Chiney was in Heidi's mouth, wriggling but unharmed. Heidi froze, unsure what to do. Sandy shouted, "Leave it, leave it, Heidi!" And Heidi, trusting her mom's voice more than her own instincts, gently released Chiney. The squirrel bolted up the trunk and vanished into the branches where her family waited.

Rusty was always present during Heidi's hunting fits, but he never tried to catch one himself. He seemed content to play the role of dignified observer.

You'd think Chiney might learn her lesson—but she didn't. On another occasion, she ran along the top of the park fence, nimble and defiant, with Rusty and Heidi in hot pursuit, eyes locked on her from below. Just as she aimed for the oak tree, Heidi intercepted her mid-run. Unbelievably, Chiney flipped into the air—a daring move that distracted the dogs just long enough for her to escape. She was so fast, she could even confuse Heidi now and then.

When it was time to go home, Sandy would call them in. Rusty would give his usual bark, nudging Heidi for one last round of chase, a drink of water, and then—satisfied and spent—they'd head home together.

From high in the oak tree, Chiney watched them go. Her tail flicked with mischief, eyes bright and alert. She hadn't learned her lesson—she'd simply been biding her time. The next chase was already brewing.

The coyote

One evening, around 7:40 p.m.—about an hour before sunset—Art and Sandy took the kids for a walk around their neighborhood, a quiet circle of homes. Each walked one dog, strolling side by side in a relaxed rhythm.

Then, at about fifteen feet ahead, a mid-sized coyote emerged from between two houses, stepping into view as if crossing a threshold between worlds. It paused, halfway across the street, and looked directly at them.

Art, Sandy, Rusty, and Heidi all stopped instinctively. No one spoke. The air felt still.

Rusty and Heidi sat quietly, not barking or lunging, but watching with a kind of solemn curiosity. Though the creature resembled a dog, something in its bearing told them otherwise. It was wild—not a friend, not a foe, but something ancient and untamed. And they knew it.

The coyote, unbothered by their presence, stood with the confidence of one who belonged. It held their gaze for a moment longer, then turned and continued on its path, disappearing between the houses as silently as it had arrived.

Sandy and Art watched the coyote move with quiet authority, and something stirred in them—a recognition of instinct, of boundaries, of the silent language animals speak when they know they're not alone.

Al's Visit

Al had found the job of his dreams in a city in South Florida. The salary was good, though the hours were long. Still, one day he announced he'd be visiting the following weekend. When Rusty saw him walk through the door, his joy was boundless. Heidi followed close behind, eager to join in the fun the two boys shared during Al's short visit.

Later, as Al sat with Art and Sandy exchanging news and stories, Rusty rested calmly by his feet. Heidi lay on the other side, ready for pats and attention. Al asked about Rusty's early mischief—was he still stealing Daddy's socks from the laundry? Still untying Sandy's shoelaces? The answer was no. He'd outgrown those habits. He was more mature now.

"How about neutering and spaying?" Al asked.

"Yep," Sandy replied. "They both went through it."

Rusty had worn shorts to protect his healing area and had slowed down his play for a while. Heidi, whose surgery included the repair of an abdominal hernia, was back to playing by that same evening— and every day after that. Typical Heidi: surgery in the morning, zoomies by night.

Al leaned against the doorway, watching Heidi parade around with a sock in her mouth like it was royal regalia.

"And I suppose, just like 'Papito,' Heidi is now 'Mamita,' huh?" he said, grinning.

"You got it," Sandy replied. "That's our go-to name for every beloved lady—two-legged or four."

The kids giggled. Heidi dropped the sock and barked once, as if to confirm her title.

"Is Rusty still the champion of kisses? Does he shower Heidi with them too?"

"Oh, he adores kissing Heidi. She's not a fan, but she's learned to put up with his smooches—most of the time."

Al had to return home that Sunday but promised to visit again. He needed to see the kids in person—after all, they couldn't hear him on the phone the way Art and Sandy could.

Some friendships don't end—they simply keep walking beside you.

Always, Forever Friends

On walks through the winding paths of their community, Sandy or Art would sometimes spot Dixie being walked by her dad. Rusty always saw her first—his eyes lighting up the moment she came into view. Without hesitation, he'd run to greet his forever friend.

Dixie, just as thrilled, would spin in delight and meet him halfway. The two would tumble into play, wrestling and romping like they had in their younger days, as if no time had passed at all.

Heidi adored Dixie from the very beginning. Anyone Rusty loved, she welcomed with open paws. The three of them—Rusty, Heidi, and Dixie—would reunite on holidays and special walks, their joy unmistakable, their bond unbreakable.

They didn't need words. Their friendship was written in movement, in shared glances, in the rhythm of paws on pavement. It was the kind of connection that doesn't fade with time.

Because real friends—true friends—are always, forever friends.

Sandy would sometimes pause and watch them from a few steps behind, her heart full. In their joy, she saw something rare and lasting—an unspoken promise of loyalty, of love without conditions. And in those moments, she knew: she was witnessing something sacred.

AMOR Y AMISTAD

VERSIÓN ESPAÑOL DISPONIBLE

www.ingramcontent.com/pod-product-compliance
Lightning Source LLC
Chambersburg PA
CBHW051646120626
46551CB00015B/2241